CONTINUOUS FRIEZE BORDERING RED

POETS OUT LOUD))) Elisabeth Frost, *series editor*

CONTINUOUS FRIEZE

Michelle Naka Pierce

BORDERING RED

Fordham University Press • NEW YORK 2012

Copyright © 2012 Fordham University Press.

All rights reserved. No part of this publication may be reproduced, stored in a retrieval system, or transmitted in any form or by any means— electronic, mechanical, photocopy, recording, or any other—except for brief quotations in printed reviews, without the prior permission of the publisher.

Fordham University Press has no responsibility for the persistence or accuracy of URLs for external or third-party Internet websites referred to in this publication and does not guarantee that any content on such websites is, or will remain, accurate or appropriate.

Fordham University Press also publishes its books in a variety of electronic formats. Some content that appears in print may not be available in electronic books.

Library of Congress Cataloging-in-Publication Data is available from the publisher.

Printed in the United States of America
14 13 12   5 4 3 2 1   FIRST EDITION

for Chris and Fairholme

ACKNOWLEDGMENTS

Grateful acknowledgment to Susana Gardner and the Dusie Kollektiv; a short excerpt of this book was published as a chapbook: *Symptom of Color* (Dusie, 2011). Thank you to the editors of *Bombay Gin* in which earlier versions of some of this work previously appeared.

Love and thanks to Chris Pusateri, Yasamin Ghiasi, Sue Hammond West, Bhanu Kapil, Andrew Wille, Gabrielle Civil, and Michiko Masuda Pierce for their support. Appreciation to Naropa University for the generous subvention to support the use of the cover art and for granting a sabbatical leave, during which I moved to London, attended the Rothko exhibit at the Tate Modern, and conceived of this project.

Much gratitude to everyone at Fordham University Press, especially Elisabeth Frost, Helen Tartar, Janet Kaplan, Thomas Lay, Eric Newman, Molly Dorozenski, Katie Sweeney, Kate O'Brien-Nicholson, Loomis Mayer, Andrea Shahan, Jonathan Coppola, and Mei-mei Berssenbrugge. Appreciation to Rachel Blau DuPlessis, Kass Fleisher, and Timothy Yu for their thoughtful attention to the work. Finally, a special thank you to the Rothko Estate, the Artists Rights Society, and the Tate Modern for use of Mark Rothko's Seagram mural as cover art: *Black on Maroon*, 1959.

I realize that historically the function of painting large pictures is painting something very grandiose and pompous. The reason I paint them, however . . . is precisely because I want to be very intimate and human. To paint a small picture is to place yourself outside your experience, to look upon it with a reducing glass. However you paint the larger picture, you are in it. It isn't something you command.

MARK ROTHKO

I am other to myself precisely at the place where I expect to be myself.

JUDITH BUTLER

This is an inauspicious way to begin, inside your country bolt on, oxygen feeding the cellular white. As [elapsed turquoise] around the wrinkled eye. Tourists here are on a steady diet of art consumption, and non-breathable sweaters. Referred pain emerges in the shoul[der] behind the scapula: you are left with You confuse the other word for carrot with the other word for onion. You don't know the difference languages taste, though "synthetic" comes to mind. Self-portrait transfer. You arrive on a Thursday or you sleep metaphorically, you try to understand the dorsal aspect of the body. Though not your first the museum now resembles an all-you-can-eat buffet. How can you correct your traveler-status if you the imprint of a dying father who appears in a navy suit beneath a nascent oak. Can you monitor between the other words for mushrooms and yam noodles. Your codes compressed in synapses. Skin a Monday. In the morning or in the awful night. You anticipate the worst as you approach customs:

crossing, you are on the outside, inside this once removed zone, just beyond the city. Underground you only have a finite time of existence, if you don't understand how gas converts to liquid? Condensation the changes? Molecular shifts visible to the eye if you only knew how to look closely. Energy, down. lighter than. Darker than. A tint off. Lemons squeezed to bleach the tissue [flash]. The hue: all consuming the lines, the interrogation, the sullied plexiglas. Exchange rates are alarming, and each time you purchase hear languages not easily recognized, and the sounds are muffled, as though submerged. All around

takes on new significance, as you unpack not only your things but your national identity, which is

Pictures of the human figure alone in a moment of utter immobility. Pixilated. Spiraled. A wave of

in this delusion you call continuance. A border is not clean. When the tape is removed, the paint has

something, you must convert amounts into dollars to understand their worth. Everything becomes

citizens rush to their destinations, minding gaps and such. You are caught between two lines, wondering
already in a state of flux from an ethnic standpoint. Distance plays tricks on your perception. From afar,
rejection. You find yourself not in the mood for encapsulated life—that is, to be boxed in by the frames.
seeped under, forced in by the brush. In script, you find a speck of resistance. Or a malleable conflict.
suspect. You delight in regional nuances, the way prepositions shift in usage. Or how six inches of snow

what it means to give good service. Here, the delivery matches your own. Burning decks within an

it looks as though the entire canvas wasn't used, but up close, you see beige paint and hope this isn't idle

Something about this afternoon says dance. This drizzle. Repetition. A variation where you enter

You are being pulled under, only you cannot go there, not today, where the tributary is harsh and divides

can crumble an infrastructure. If only you were here at the turn of the last century. No documents were

[un]familiar territory. Patrons, patriots, deserters alike turn the wheels in order to move along the tracks commentary on your life. You hear your text [a taxonomy of cultural products] translated into another the scroll. Your moniker not to be worn out with the years. The mere will to act is primitive. Can you the city. You are thinking of the degrading banks. The intense indigos and maroons. From your needed then to get a library card. You are tagged on the back of a used envelope. Glue deteriorates:

and import substance. You'd like to open up, as if a tunnel could part out of nowhere, allowing you to language and find it's like being introduced to yourself in the mirror, only you don't recognize that it's enumerate the lacerations wearing out the day? Y e l l o w e c h o. Can you locate the inverse of peripheral vision, you feel you could skip into the pockets [into the shadowy glass] and disappear. But decreasing the value of membranes. Yet the ink stains remain contained: you are careful not to smear or pass through a mountain, but the accent [your own] creates some invisible words. You are not alone on you. Who is this broker between forms and documents, not evenly in between? This is your plight, potential tension? V e n e t i a n r e d. Lay your head down on this ceramic makura as ojiichan once did. you do not. Nothing is inert or dormant. Not these borders that float. Not the one your mother crossed. blemish the flap. This morning you wake to precipitation and soon learn that repeating phrases [even this journey, and sometimes there are no opportunities to breathe. The carbon dioxide increases and

which reminds you that moving from one country to another just after birth doesn't allow for roots to set

Only the altitude has changed. You appear more interested in the behavior surrounding the film than

Not this unexpected passage where you must step outside [into everything] into this new unknown.

slowly] doesn't make them any less foreign to your ear. You ask a local to pronounce something confuses the brain. Without friends in the vicinity, you've taken up talking to yourself and taking pictures in: they are exposed, as you are, dangling from a terracotta pot. Though you are sun-marked, you are not the film itself. Distraction theory. Sense and insensitive torn from the same screen, ensna[red] by mesh. Which is an intolerable present. Which is the year your father dies. You get caught between dreams and to make sure that the final letter is silent: "yes, we eat the end of our words." Definitions continue to on the street. You think the image allows for solace; indeed it allows for angst. Unconnected to your taiyo rising. Nor do you contemplate the sac[red] obligations of the zia's four winds. As the daughter of Now all you can see is violence: a hand dragged in anthropomorphic dross. Curved. It's autumn all at waking life. Many nights in a row, he is there, though he never speaks. And you feel the wound and the confuse in much the same way that you resemble an outcast. Integration renovates the hybrid's wiring alphabet, silence occupies the snapshots. Your speech pattern slows way-the-fuck-down against identity an immigrant, you've had barriers established for you. Not by your mother necessarily, but the union. once, or it's the middle of spring. Mourning leaves you stagnant. A period, for instance: a kind of death. invisible grief. The indistinct edges of sorrow and sadness. Water spilling, damaging the words. Symbols while leaving the façade more or less intact. "You are as white as a non-white girl can get." Or: "In this

theft. No one wants to pay an idiom tax, but the bills keep coming. Hold yourself underwater, placed
Not the union exactly, but the war and the occupation that followed. How to be eastern when due west,
And so you decide [actually you grasp] that you must keep moving. In the first month, you board a plane.
washed out by a flood. "You are born only once with this name," but your mother says this to your
moment, you seem very Asian to me." One district deterritorializes as you chart another. Channel.

ever so gently in the hand, like an uncompromising narrative. Like an epistle extracted from a travel line. when at the top of the hill in this 18-mile city that sets in burnt orange. Sand devils kicked up in the eyes. In the sixth, you learn the forces of flight: lift, drag, thrust, and weight. Apropos of nothing, you reiterate partner and not to you. What does it mean to construct "experience" out of photo or note? Memories are Polyglot hermeneutics or a stitch by stitch enunciation. Line of escape. You turn toward your extremities:

When a nervous twitch begins again in the inner ear, you wonder whether motion sickness is a loss of The fringe a forgotten setting. Driving up Route 66 and blinded by a disc that has increased in size. All that you have never been "white girl pretty" but have been the object of Asiaphiles. This gives you no muted during re-entry. Dialects once recognizable, now strange. A reverse culture shock. You must ambiguous trimmings and mixed-up past: here, over there, everything between. In the end, you need equilibrium or a loss of self. The dislocation. The relocation. The problem of location itself. The you want to do is step on the gas of your Datsun pick-up and slam it into a concrete wall or dump it comfort. You locate [situate yourself against] the idea of beauty in a culture that does not value your scrutinize the canal and cochlea to consider voices heard over digital airwaves. As a hammer strikes a diagram to find the resting places of everyone you know. The space is opening up, and you find it depiction arrives in the blood—vein toward, artery away. The ground is shifting, quite literally, and into an arroyo. There are breakages in the conversion of romaji. Change is likely to underscore little currency: dimples for knuckles [inversion]. Here and abroad, which becomes another here [but not for and rebounds, strings continue at their resonant frequency. Acoustics released. Some think that frightening. Tectonic plates adjust with prompt disruption. Then surge: triggering this border response a nomad existence is not what you crave. You miss a day, or part of a day, and find intensity in difference. Be prepared. Out of kindness comes redness; however, repression isn't always marked by you]. Internalized oppression penetrates the casing and confiscates reason so that there is nothing but "border incident" is war, but it's also when you cross yourself, back track along a preliminary direction [alert: orange]. Right angles indicate barriers and fragility. The inside of commotion. The inside of the [im]balance, in the absence that someone [somewhere] calls survival. Much of your time is spent intention. It is even more hurt than that. A single image. Copper, dust, and this damn rainy city, which center with your skin on the outskirts. How does the offspring assimilate? Interweave the various and lose your way. When you can no longer stand under the deluge of selves. When the idea of home thoughts you didn't realize were yours [aka: hibernation]. The body is so full [of pain, of more internal examining little movements, between center and cinder, for instance. So much for the era of quantified reminds you of your mother's, in which you will always be a gaijin or yank [in both]. The tenor, backlit. conditions? You are thinking about the gingerroot, as you prepare sustenance [read: provisions for becomes absorbed, then deposited along the riverbed. Sediment. Erosion and abrasion. What is the variation] that it begins to vibrate, shattering the container that encloses it. Or not. Not shatter, which

> As oxygen is taken in, eight sharp breaths.
> You are nowhere near this tint in pattern,
> nowhere near the agitation.

phonemes. For the first time, or maybe not, you begin to feel your age—in the arch, Achilles, and left fin. You are other overcoming otherness. You are different in the corners under the same shade, under a the journey]. You do not have the luxury of cleansing your palate between bites of raw fish, not along impact on the itinerant body? A shifting present. An assortment of venues: Rio Grande, Nueces River, implies breaking into pieces. More like dispersion. Water pellets moving across a hard exterior until they

        Autumn is held isolate: indistinct edge
                    against the edge of inquiry. You decelerate to reconcile the geographies,
                                to reverse periodic segments that reiterate grief.

In the unexamined clinamen. As if the focal point were always in motion or absent from conversation. As protested focus. Your self-exam reveals a macula, which may be the result of age or the result of crisis. these lateral shoots, which demand rapid change. So you grate over meat and vegetables, skin and all, Edo Bay. You desire singularity, but notions of a fixed point destabilize. Soon a horizon of expectation evaporate. A fountain of mercury or change in ocular migraine. This glass so slick that it does not absorb

        In this language: a shaking of the trees
[both occupied and empty]   identified
          through columns of bare silhouette. The [dis]advantage
               of a sentence not worth closing.

if the circumference were able to result in an amicable divorce. You meet everyone you know in letters or And even if you could be any dark formation, even in the most necessary of installments, your life and hope not to nick your knuckles. Faulty [red]uction. The border is a scar on the forearm. Is emerges: the equivalent of a rupture [rapture]. And you begin to embrace your incongruent parts, to [no stomal gate]. You are this continuous sequence with adjacent elements not perceptibly different.

Soon you will deliberate the murky pale,
that viscous substance in exposed heart.
                Unlike any cerebral moment,   it is possible for the present
                to influence the past. To influence the b l a c k e n e d s u r f a c e.

at the long syllable's edge: to foreground the aspirated consonants, the dripping vowels. The page is wet, discriminates against it. Depression. This month, this time of year, this climate. Any spectacle is a conversation with your naturalized mother or white partner. Is the syllable added in the transliteration sketch a shelter out of fragments. Your "struggle is to see [and be seen] from both perspectives at once." Assassinate. Little more little. Repeat instruction. Instead of faulting yourself for going outside the lines,

When you are seen through blind glass, it alters
the texture of what is known as [in]flexible skin.
The basic configuration of a diverted self in distressed light.

[neither][nor][both]

and moisture distorts meaning and vision. In establishing some kind of pool to wade in, you take resemblance. The expanse between the top lip and your eye makes the gouache so regular. Mending of your name. For protection, you begin an epistolary trek to search for a recognizable self. Sporadic The afterimage fades. Your eyelids are thinner than you think: see-through. Iguana no musume. you integrate the veer. A cultural trace is repetition [imitating your mother's salty palms as they shape

In the absence of an accurate reflection,   a [red]acted identity ensues.
               You rotate without spotting   and focus inward.
Forgotten: the basic sequences of steps.
               One two three three four.   Vertigo.

the place of the name. Or the name takes the place of you. Then resides inside your mouth, between
the imbalance does not. Winter glides along the force of sacrifice. All room in shadow. The immigrant is
morsels in the notebook. Then choking. As your cells readjust to the lack of solar warmth and the
The weather has picked up, but you do not attempt to describe the temperature. Arms stretched across a
onigiri]. But also a swerve from the original, a deviation in trajectory marking atomic turbulence. Can you

       It is difficult to renew cells,
              as you acquaint yourself with a counter narrative.
              As though the slit in retina came before all saturation.

cheek and gum, to avoid getting chewed up by questions. Your vocabulary tremors, so you tape the seen as exotic, but the offspring ugly and deformed, except when a child. Then neighborhood teenage meridian air and an abundance of moisture, which collects on the sill and coats the black stairwell down frame, seeking three elements [not dead center] in a viewfinder. Color peels off its object. Separation is begin with this shift: see yourself as *different*, not as *illegitimate*, to reverse the vibrations and their effects.

Do not utterly engage.   Time anchors left then repeats.
Then infuses your excavated veins.
Insofar as some thing that could not endure.

window [a giant X from corner to corner] to protect against earthquakes, though you've yet to experience girls want to walk you around the block in a stroller, as though you were a doll, which gives you to your flat. The notion of the anterior pure [junsui] is a construct, but the hybrid offspring [zasshu] has difficult under any degree of order. Passing into this port. A demarcation, where this sentence ends and What might be more likely than singularity to take separation. Clemency. The price of persuasion in

The problem was to image an image.   To make a place   rather than vestiges.
To acquiesce to the muddled storm [mysteriously elongated].
                    Wherein the false bricked-in windows
                              left your interior pervasive.

one here. Never is there a time for a rehearsal of blue. See Mediterranean. See perpetual surface. You reoccurring nightmares about being kidnapped. They want to strip you of your clothes [when you are difficulty observing this. Your body doesn't understand "less internal variation." It absorbs the pejorative this line begins with a reverberation. And so it is about what happens before this moment and what pliable joy. Is the sever mostly decision? A line distinguished. The lexicon includes echoes and belongs,

Other[s] are made for nowhere.
Are [un]made   in compelling strangeness.
                      You surrender to the cuts   between,
                      to the internal markings   of sympathetic ink.

cannot inhabit the non-tourist space fully and consequently find yourself examining the benefits of twelve] in a utility room where no one will see. In this unkempt sentence, in this lattice of vagueness, connotations cultivated in your saliva. While your stock does not lead to inbreeding, it does not yield happens after, but what of the moment itself? How do you attempt being human, when prior to this, you not to you, but to the structure of utterance. You unthread the hem: reconfigure the shades between reds.

You must acknowledge this scar tissue and proceed.

Dare penetrable red.

inertia: questioning whether it exerts strength. A corridor fully magnified may complete the kinetic pitch, lies violence. Stain upon stain upon tender withering letter. You are an ordinary color. A neglected "refinement" or "conventionalization" of traditions either. The placement of your left hand is corrected are often reminded you are not. Human. You're a paper creature constructed out of what seems like All this to indicate a displacement of spectral lines toward wavelengths [the velocity of recession].

This is a time of transition,				a threshold.
Yet the architecture cannot be seen from this angle.

but outside the desert is lack of sun and lack of sky. If objects contain the infinite, then you are only Tuesday. A notable degree of claret in immaterial exchange. Just as you are suffering, you read yourself: as you eat gohan with your right. The hybrid is crude with unrefined manners, regardless of heterosis. predetermined folds. You'd like to unfurl. To proceed beyond the creases that dictate future steps. To White surrounds you. Your presence in this absence detracts and complicates the sensation of emptiness.

a shade of red. Narrow, like this room you call a flat. You call a 9 x 13 box. You call home [in quotation the whole center and the circumference in hanging. The hybrid offspring cannot culturally reproduce. Indeed: you have "more internal variation," and as a result, more vibration: this oscillation of cultural consider what preceded the pleat. A doubling back to commence again. Each day a separate impulse. As each stitch is ripped, you are careful not to mar any adjacent fabric. That is, a perforated edge still marks]. Again, you make a list, crave some semblance of forecast. In other words, thirst approximates

You are missing DNA. This way of dressing is an offering, which is not the same as disappearance.

components, leaving your equilibrium disturbed. Displacement ensues as you cross time zones to embark

Intransitive verbs on display with compass in error. Engulfed in a sordid pulp. [Infraction: a failure to

exists: o n c e a b o r d e r h e r e. You [red]raw the line, using soap as your mother would, to re-baste water. How the body yields in descriptive mode and harnesses speech in order to point and define the There is pleasure when there is passage. When there is room. When it is open. Entrance. No window is a new continent. Sight becomes distorted. A clot occurs in the temporal lobe, and you seep into that comply with undocumented reference.] Initially, unbeknownst to you, there is a subtle rift between you the gash. Irreparably flawed and not. You step outside this season to recover the delineated space and margins. While oxygen is taken in, a nebula appears: trace the pattern so the anxiety held can dissipate. futile even if obscured. You are not that which is not white. But then again, maybe you are. Here a box sticky mass. You desire to soothe the discoloration, the wall of red, the lack of breathing room when and your immigrant mother and an unintentional alignment with your citizen father. [Concealed topography of features. Anxiety builds in the temple, in the pulse, so you practice wrist compression

A visceral reaction occurs along the cervical vertebrae, where C4 through C7 protrude, exposing containing a drape is sentimental usage. You've experienced countless years of separation. A single you stand inside searching for exits, which are painted over [they do not open]. Someone, somewhere assimilation due to site-specific development.] To mend the fault lines, you examine the bruises. You are during re-entry. The site of losing bearings during a rough landing. You attend to the blood pumping to a vulnerable contact point. Is the backdrop an indication of your homeland? The hues rise, and you

scientific statement at dusk. No question, there is regret. You'd do well to get yourself out of this sodden

must understand the loss and the shallow water that hovers. This morning there is snow: greyness that

only present as an indecipherable mark, lacking particular function. How do you navigate the tarnished

your ears by tapping three fingers on your sternum. Pain and comfort simultaneously. A pathology arises visualize [quite unexpectedly] a scene where red meets yellow meets sky. Scatter effect. You are with your weather into an arid region into an open field of unbroken surface, notwithstanding any unforeseen covers the sky and as extension the mind. You are thinking about murals these days and how to address arteries? No need to be coy with supervision afoot [in sexy boot]. To wear out lenses is to shutter, with inflight semantics. Things on the outside trespass in, forcing things on the inside out. The molecules partner, yet nowhere near, and the two of you find restrictions within the function of in[ter]dependence. status change. Under your breath you let out an expletive: fuck the hyphen. Then louder. Fucking the unstable border. You spend your time abstracting: a gloss of ochre spreads across, layer after layer; exploiting simple accidents or flaws. Things haven't happened yet, though the driftwood's suspended. in your cells move at high speeds so that when the context unveils itself, you can fit in. Peripatetic.

It is the aperture that has the potential to translate this movement from your origin[s]. You are living hyphen. Can you translate authority? You do not identify as combined words, linked grammar, division the frame turns and paint drips in multiple directions. This is how one navigates new geographical Everywhere a camera, netting your prayers. April is here and outside are disposable buttercups. It is No resting on the tarmac for you. You are finally breaking down any [mis]perceived symmetry.

what some call a polycontinental transexperience. Only no one really calls it that. Racial fluidity, as you of recognized sloth. You are not some checked box on a limited census form. There is no dash between locations. Not directionless: polyvectorial. A plane flies overhead. You are mere minutes from a runway the liminal recognized in trellis. The scarring with an edge predicament. These seasons gather speed, then Destroying nations of [self] [other] [inside] [out]. You used to know your range through someone else's.

know it, is a myth. At night you exist in suggestions of carmine, a displacement occurs. REM. The outer

Japanese and American, nor after your middle name. Which means just that: center, middle, inside.

and are reminded of travel, not physical shifts, but cultural ones. The way a recipe must alter its

disperse to extend an architectonic form. Autumn is enormous this time of winter. Boundaries: they exist

This color which is not one. Which is not monochromatic intensity. Estranged: searching for overlapping limit of each zone is not a concept familiar to the fluids you carry. As if concentric circles in pebble-pond The care with which the rain is wrong inside this cavity. Inside the reddening of visage, inside nuance, ing[red]ients when made on various coordinates. No access to a particular vegetable or herb: you do not on maps. You run into them when you submit your passport. You are annoyed when you are chosen for elements. Now you are disruptive and productive [in tandem]. You terrorize the unp[red]ictable scene.

theory are at once put into practice. Disappearance. That is, the self *feels* static, then not. Then seemingly inside this alarming evening. You make a timetable of when to eat, shit, and catch the train, but never is own a nabemono to make sukiyaki, for instance. And one generation's palate [palette] is different from a random search, and the things in your bags are taken out one by one and then haphazardly stuffed back There is no place, really, where you are not alien. But you are studying the cadence of passing from side static again. The environment, what with all the rain, deposits trace minerals, causing the dreaded there enough time to pack. Because how do you know what to bring as you meet yourself in another the next. A portion of your tongue [or the roof of your mouth] is excised. You can no longer speak in. You fear them when [after you have written that you are a professor on a declaration card] you are to side, the grammar of intricate mobility. Some days you feel remote. The company you keep is solitary.

ephemeral syndrome. You are in place and displaced simultaneously. The result of being horizontal in country—especially when you feel that you haven't quite met yourself in your own. Seizures adjust the original text, so instead you build a copy. You can no longer taste the subtle flavor of sticky white asked, "What is it that you profess?" Checkpoints are real and insistent and at other times rather benign. It is difficult to consider intervals inhabited by another. You desire. This. You do not desire. This.

a vertical city. Although you desire various markers [brown desert with a touch of sagebrush, the peaks themselves for an alligator-cracked finish. While you sit on the three-tiered bleacher, you observe rice and are ashamed, sitting across your mother with apologetic longing. When you enter the exhibit, Your sense of direction is confused by this. Single color in an arrangement of equation and not ordinary. Accordingly, you hope this itinerary will provide some ease. Not resolution, but temporary relief from of the continental divide], the terrain here asks you to literally map the fractals that occur naturally. the tendencies of [some] women at a makeup table. Light changes your mood. A mirror is held, but you you read: "to give this space." But you find there are limitations even within that. The confines are There were no rooms, but room and a limit. A kind of moss growing between. There was an occupation, the constellations of discourse acquisition. Indigenous to neither, you remain ainoko. Given that you

Consider the snowflake, an ice crystal with delicate six-fold symmetry. How can you convey the floating are not in the reflection. Arms from nowhere comb your hair. One day your clothes will be manufactured invisible but present [i.e., enforceable]. No one will check your visa. Your accent, however, will be and the space within was a space within. There were few to occupy the remains of an offering. The way have trouble encoding and retrieving memories, you've begun to make things up. What the brain will do border [not floating world] and its edges, which are sometimes smudged sometimes translucent feathers, from obsolete maps. A child [a hybrid in her own right] performs down dog and smiles; you watch this questioned. Hard Gs. Hard Fs. Not to mention your inability to bow properly when meeting strangers on a voiceprint creates a "missed step," one that moves along the musical staff, wraps itself up, then with trauma. Safeguard. You are somewhat afraid. Not of what exists, but of the fluctuating variables in and where does the desire for community apply? Traveling by foot circulates the blood quicker, before play out like a film. Death sits atop a white box with bloody ear and pink maw. An expression that one the street. You arrive within an unfamiliar season and have difficulty embodying the space of "I." releases. You roam these fissures and clefts: a road trip, which happens to be part train ride, which nocturnal expeditions. So much depends upon red [with rainwater] beside white. You are asked to place coagulation sets in. The taste of roasted green chile is your madeleine. Or salty compressed osembei. Can could only call sinister. Or sinful. Or simple. You arrange flowers with a towel wrapped around your Yearning: salvage and recovery. To avoid suspicion, you hover by the entry and back up against the wall: happens to be part flight. That is, the journey is startling, opening with a word rushing toward the future. a pomegranate here, to expose the pericardial sac. Each pocket holds a seed and its descendants.

you reclaim "mongrel"? Strain the semantic residue off? A slow dispersion of katakana begins. Carefully, clothes to protect your garment. An asymmetrical placement [shin, soe, hikae] is stressed to prevent still, the panels examine you. Step forward. Profile right, then left. Now move back. The threshold You are a confluence of point and counterpoint that yields and resists, that eventually looks for answers At the sight line, you hold your gaze with long approach. No incident becomes apparent until [abruptly] you examine the perforated line: a trail of confetti falls from the torn pages. Everyday someone crosses stagnation. Cut at daybreak. Maximum irrigation in the stems. You step back to question whether becomes a suture to thread. While the palette darkens, the years terminate. Despair punctures the body, in the half-rest. Progression of candor: like the metronome, whose tick hesitates just slightly to remind a detail registers. With the summer solstice immediately at your back. No eyestrain or sunspots on the perimeter. Some say invisible, but you think artificial [superimposed]. A shift toward transgressive everything is merely artificial. With only Misora Hibari in your head, you imagine nesting. Skip rope and allowing a chill to filter through. There are numerous people, but you are quite alone. Standing in the you that you do not possess this occasion. What the mind duplicates to infinity has occurred only once. future cataracts. The day concludes near midnight, when the last glimmer can be seen. Dear hybrid, perspectives, then knowledge all but collapses. Touch of slowness in the breath. The atmosphere changes become a ballet flutter. Hold yourself on sit bones, as though some thoughts for water. You try to finish interstices. Yet there is intimacy with the self. When you see red on plum on black over orange, suddenly In this subsequent viewing, there is a claustrophobic hue, which creates a new visual literacy. The dear traveler, dear subservient of red: this morning is like any morning. The snow crests the mountain during descent: pulls in high-pressure air and creates a vacuum. How is it that you are able to walk freely a seam your mother started: you lay each segment down, one after another, and request equal weight, but purple and brown appear. A silver haze. Squares inside rectangles inside squares and suddenly electrical doorway flanks the left 24 inches of one painting and the right 24 of another. That pale blue wall in the distant west. The air is crisp, but soon it will be filled with heat. The letter hasn't arrived yet:

about the cabin while others risk [der]ision at the hands of Metro station announcers? Your skin, here in this syntax, red on red on black offers no solutions. This is an original brushstroke. Postcards are outlets and heating radiators materialize. Followed by soft edges, blurry. Like water damage. You are that between two maroons [so deep in their tone]: earth on either side of water. Each time you step, even if or only in pieces. You are waiting in the long line that is called the sentence: in the ubiquitous fragment, in the end, is a similar shade of foreign. A 45-minute delay due to "a person on the tracks" broadcasts transcriptions for those who understand your discomfort. Glass becomes a reflection of color not image. dot of paint. That fleck pitched by a stray bristle. No figure in the casement. The dim light determines ever so lightly, granules break away. You are this borough, straddling both sides of the canal, waiting an illegible gesture, the smudged text. That is all you can do. You are drifting in the misunderstandings the conductor. You'd be wrong to think this wasn't an act of suicide, even though others may call it illegal You see the transition having less to do with connecting thoughts than with the migrating organism. One how you see your pallid organs, your ethnic face. There is no distance to grasp depth. This stain reflects for the swell to dissipate. Your remnants watermarked in high tide. This standing on two feet. Painting that come from distorted phrases. This letter is from a disruptive chronology, an alternate timeline.

immigration. Certainly not unlike your own excursion, yet you do have papers: [1] Slightly used passport.

moment you are upright. The next you are bent over. Suddenly a line erupts into arabesque. When you

then absorbs. And you wonder: if you cannot establish how the tessellating pieces interlock, how can you

over your own history. You become just a figure with washed out skull. An anonymous life. The shadow

Everything you say will be stolen. Folded up neatly and carried across mitigated borders: soggy

Expiry: 2018; [2] Missive from employer on letterhead, stating you *will* return to work; [3] Latchkey from point the left foot, a cramp emerges in the third and fourth digits, so you take a bite of banana to increase record it? How can you authenticate your worth? And so you must move closer then farther away in is assembled square by square in transparent logic. The measure of all things or the process of and soaked with saliva. Then the energy will be converted, as all things in this transitory life. You must your mother, worn around your neck. The still life is a small lesson on perspective. Or a large lesson

potassium levels. While a vertical stripe may represent the universe, you find your soft tissue somewhat

order to understand what it means to border the borders. The letter is an articulation, a lingering gasp.

propagating in paralysis and contour. Hands between your breasts do not indicate foreplay, but quote:

borrow the grammar of another until it becomes your own. Until this simple act becomes steady, like assembling the virtues of migration. People openly take forbidden pictures. Each time a bit of mettle is susceptible. It isn't simply pretense. It's an evocation in atmosphere through the expansive property On this particular day, you travel as the asymptote would: a line continually approaching the curve a random search. What is the value of invisibility if not invisible on the road? Forced astride this theorem an [im]pulse. You do not know which to prefer, the comfort of inflections or innuendoes. The whistling taken. You wonder if a self-portrait would disclose your various shards. The bereavement of failure. causing visual awareness. White writing records the torso or complex geometric prototypes. You're without meeting. A blinking occurs along the coast. Consumption: expenditure and waste. The tension with ID wallowing in syntax. You become a placeholder for variable signs. Not only as a metaphor that comes just before or marks each rim just after. Without describing the exact location, you pierce the

You can't remember the last time you dreamt in your mother's vernacular, so you locate pigment feeling uncomfortable in these shoes with lime stripes. With wet hair. With sweat on arms in does not lessen even with intermittent gaze. Cinch the akai mado. You forget the other word for carrot. for discovering closely guarded info about yourself [i.e., common knowledge]. You cannot describe how seasonal periphery. In the morning, when sleep is nearby, you want to understand the symptom of color.

POETS OUT LOUD
Prize Winners

Julie Choffel
The Hello Delay

Michelle Naka Pierce
Continuous Frieze Bordering Red

Leslie C. Chang
Things That No Longer Delight Me

Amy Catanzano
Multiversal

Darcie Dennigan
Corinna A-Maying the Apocalypse

Karin Gottshall
Crocus

Jean Gallagher
This Minute

Lee Robinson
Hearsay

Janet Kaplan
The Glazier's Country

Robert Thomas
Door to Door

Julie Sheehan
Thaw

Jennifer Clarvoe
Invisible Tender

www.ingramcontent.com/pod-product-compliance
Lightning Source LLC
Chambersburg PA
CBHW051214290426
44109CB00021B/2451